FOREWORD

The collection of "Everything Will Be Okay" travel phrasebooks published by T&P Books is designed for people traveling abroad for tourism and business. The phrasebooks contain what matters most - the essentials for basic communication. This is an indispensable set of phrases to "survive" while abroad.

This phrasebook will help you in most cases where you need to ask something, get directions, find out how much something costs, etc. It can also resolve difficult communication situations where gestures just won't help.

This book contains a lot of phrases that have been grouped according to the most relevant topics. You'll also find a mini dictionary with useful words - numbers, time, calendar, colors...

Take "Everything Will Be Okay" phrasebook with you on the road and you'll have an irreplaceable traveling companion who will help you find your way out of any situation and teach you to not fear speaking with foreigners.

TABLE OF CONTENTS

T&P Books Publishing

T&P Books Publishing

PHRASEBOOK
- UKRAINIAN -

By Andrey Taranov

THE MOST IMPORTANT PHRASES

This phrasebook contains
the most important
phrases and questions
for basic communication
Everything you need
to survive overseas

T&P BOOKS

Phrasebook + 250-word dictionary

English-Ukrainian phrasebook & mini dictionary

By Andrey Taranov

The collection of "Everything Will Be Okay" travel phrasebooks published by T&P Books is designed for people traveling abroad for tourism and business. The phrasebooks contain what matters most - the essentials for basic communication. This is an indispensable set of phrases to "survive" while abroad.

You'll also find a mini dictionary with 250 useful words required for everyday communication - the names of months and days of the week, measurements, family members, and more.

T&P Books Publishing
www.tpbooks.com

ISBN: 978-1-78616-745-3

This book is also available in E-book formats.
Please visit www.tpbooks.com or the major online bookstores.

PRONUNCIATION

Letter	Ukrainian example	T&P phonetic alphabet	English example

Vowels

А а	акт	[a]	shorter than in ask
Е е	берет	[e], [ɛ]	absent, pet
Є є	модельєр	[ɛ]	man, bad
И и	ритм	[k]	clock, kiss
І і	компанія	[i]	shorter than in feet
Ї ї	поїзд	[ji]	playing, spying
О о	око	[ɔ]	bottle, doctor
У у	буря	[u]	book
Ю ю	костюм	[ʲu]	cued, cute
Я я	маяк	[ja], [ʲa]	royal

Consonants

Б б	бездна	[b]	baby, book
В в	вікно	[w]	vase, winter
Г г	готель	[ɦ]	between [g] and [h]
Ґ ґ	ґудзик	[g]	game, gold
Д д	дефіс	[d]	day, doctor
Ж ж	жанр	[ʒ]	forge, pleasure
З з	зброя	[z]	zebra, please
Й й	йти	[j]	yes, New York
К к	крок	[k]	clock, kiss
Л л	лев	[l]	lace, people
М м	мати	[m]	magic, milk
Н н	назва	[n]	name, normal
П п	приз	[p]	pencil, private
Р р	радість	[r]	rice, radio
С с	сон	[s]	city, boss
Т т	тир	[t]	tourist, trip
Ф ф	фарба	[f]	face, food
Х х	холод	[h]	home, have
Ц ц	церква	[ts]	cats, tsetse fly
Ч ч	час	[tʃ]	church, French

Letter	Ukrainian example	T&P phonetic alphabet	English example
Ш ш	шуба	[ʃ]	machine, shark
Щ щ	щука	[ɕ]	sheep, shop
ь	камінь	[ʲ]	soft sign - no sound
ъ	ім'я	[ʲ]	hard sign, no sound

LIST OF ABBREVIATIONS

English abbreviations

ab.	-	about
adj	-	adjective
adv	-	adverb
anim.	-	animate
as adj	-	attributive noun used as adjective
e.g.	-	for example
etc.	-	et cetera
fam.	-	familiar
fem.	-	feminine
form.	-	formal
inanim.	-	inanimate
masc.	-	masculine
math	-	mathematics
mil.	-	military
n	-	noun
pl	-	plural
pron.	-	pronoun
sb	-	somebody
sing.	-	singular
sth	-	something
v aux	-	auxiliary verb
vi	-	intransitive verb
vi, vt	-	intransitive, transitive verb
vt	-	transitive verb

Ukrainian abbreviations

ж	-	feminine noun
мн	-	plural
с	-	neuter
ч	-	masculine noun

UKRAINIAN PHRASEBOOK

This section contains
important phrases that may
come in handy in various
real-life situations.
The phrasebook will help
you ask for directions, clarify
a price, buy tickets, and
order food at a restaurant

T&P Books Publishing

PHRASEBOOK
CONTENTS

T&P Books Publishing

The bare minimum

Excuse me, ...	**Вибачте, ...** ['wɨbatʃtɛ, ...]
Hello.	**Добрий день.** ['dɔbrɨj dɛnʲ.]
Thank you.	**Дякую.** ['dʲakuʲu.]
Good bye.	**До побачення.** [do po'batʃɛnʲa.]
Yes.	**Так.** [tak.]
No.	**Ні.** [ni.]
I don't know.	**Я не знаю.** [ja nɛ 'znaʲu.]
Where? | Where to? | When?	**Де? | Куди? | Коли?** [dɛ? | ku'dɨ? | ko'lɨ?]
I need ...	**Мені потрібен ...** [mɛ'ni po'tribɛn ...]
I want ...	**Я хочу ...** [ja 'hɔtʃu ...]
Do you have ...?	**У вас є ...?** [u was 'ɛ ...?]
Is there a ... here?	**Тут є ...?** [tut ɛ ...?]
May I ...?	**Чи можна мені ...?** [tʃɨ 'mɔʒna mɛ'ni ...?]
..., please (polite request)	**Будь ласка** [budʲ 'laska]
I'm looking for ...	**Я шукаю ...** [ja ʃu'kaʲu ...]
restroom	**туалет** [tua'lɛt]
ATM	**банкомат** [banko'mat]
pharmacy (drugstore)	**аптеку** [ap'tɛku]
hospital	**лікарню** [li'karnʲu]
police station	**поліцейську дільницю** [poli'tsɛjsʲku dilʲ'nɨtsʲu]
subway	**метро** [mɛt'rɔ]

taxi	**таксі** [tak'si]
train station	**вокзал** [wok'zal]

My name is ...	**Мене звуть ...** [mɛ'nɛ zwutʲ ...]
What's your name?	**Як вас звуть?** [jak was 'zwutʲ?]
Could you please help me?	**Допоможіть мені, будь ласка.** [dopomo'ʒitʲ mɛ'ni, budʲ 'laska.]
I've got a problem.	**У мене проблема.** [u 'mɛnɛ prob'lɛma.]
I don't feel well.	**Мені погано.** [mɛ'ni po'ɦano.]
Call an ambulance!	**Викличте швидку!** ['wɨklɨt͡ʃtɛ ʃwɨd'ku!]
May I make a call?	**Чи можна мені зателефонувати?** [t͡ʃɨ 'mɔʒna mɛ'ni zatɛlɛfonu'watɨ?]

I'm sorry.	**Прошу вибачення** ['prɔʃu 'wɨbat͡ʃɛnʲa]
You're welcome.	**Прошу** ['prɔʃu]

I, me	**я** [ja]
you (inform.)	**ти** [tɨ]
he	**він** [win]
she	**вона** [wo'na]
they (masc.)	**вони** [wo'nɨ]
they (fem.)	**вони** [wo'nɨ]
we	**ми** [mɨ]
you (pl)	**ви** [wɨ]
you (sg, form.)	**Ви** [wɨ]

ENTRANCE	**ВХІД** [whid]
EXIT	**ВИХІД** ['wɨhid]
OUT OF ORDER	**НЕ ПРАЦЮЄ** [nɛ pra'tsʲuɛ]
CLOSED	**ЗАКРИТО** [za'krito]

OPEN	**ВІДКРИТО** [wid'krіto]
FOR WOMEN	**ДЛЯ ЖІНОК** [dlʲa ʒi'nɔk]
FOR MEN	**ДЛЯ ЧОЛОВІКІВ** [dlʲa tʃolowi'kiw]

Questions

Where?	**Де?** [dɛ?]
Where to?	**Куди?** [ku'dɨ?]
Where from?	**Звідки?** ['zwidkɨ?]
Why?	**Чому?** [ʧo'mu?]
For what reason?	**Навіщо?** [na'wiço?]
When?	**Коли?** [ko'lɨ?]

How long?	**Скільки часу?** ['skilʲkɨ 'ʧasu?]
At what time?	**О котрій?** [o kot'rij?]
How much?	**Скільки коштує?** ['skilʲkɨ 'koʃtuɛ?]
Do you have ...?	**У вас є ...?** [u was 'ɛ ...?]
Where is ...?	**Де знаходиться ...?** [dɛ zna'hɔdɨtʲsʲa ...?]

What time is it?	**Котра година?** [ko'tra ɦo'dɨna?]
May I make a call?	**Чи можна мені зателефонувати?** [ʧɨ 'moʒna mɛ'ni zatɛlɛfonu'watɨ?]
Who's there?	**Хто там?** [hto tam?]
Can I smoke here?	**Чи можна мені тут палити?** [ʧɨ 'moʒna mɛ'ni tut pa'lɨtɨ?]
May I ...?	**Чи можна мені ...?** [ʧɨ 'moʒna mɛ'ni ...?]

Needs

I'd like …	**Я б хотів /хотіла/ …** [ja b ho'tiw /ho'tila/ …]
I don't want …	**Я не хочу …** [ja nɛ 'hɔʧu …]
I'm thirsty.	**Я хочу пити.** [ja 'hɔʧu 'piti.]
I want to sleep.	**Я хочу спати.** [ja 'hɔʧu 'spati.]

I want …	**Я хочу …** [ja 'hɔʧu …]
to wash up	**вмитися** ['wmitisʲa]
to brush my teeth	**почистити зуби** [po'ʧistiti 'zubɨ]
to rest a while	**трохи відпочити** ['trɔhɨ widpo'ʧiti]
to change my clothes	**переодягнутися** [pɛrɛodʲaɦ'nutisʲa]

to go back to the hotel	**повернутися в готель** [powɛr'nutisʲa w ɦo'tɛlʲ]
to buy …	**купити …** [ku'piti …]
to go to …	**з'їздити в …** ['zʲizditi w …]
to visit …	**відвідати …** [wid'widati …]
to meet with …	**зустрітися з …** [zust'ritisʲa z …]
to make a call	**зателефонувати** [zatɛlɛfonu'wati]

I'm tired.	**Я втомився /втомилася/.** [ja wto'miwsʲa /wto'miɫasʲa/.]
We are tired.	**Ми втомилися.** [mɨ wto'miɫisʲa.]
I'm cold.	**Мені холодно.** [mɛ'ni 'hɔlodno.]
I'm hot.	**Мені спекотно.** [mɛ'ni spɛ'kɔtno.]
I'm OK.	**Мені нормально.** [mɛ'ni nor'malʲno.]

I need to make a call.

Мені треба зателефонувати.
[mɛ'ni 'trɛba zatɛlɛfonu'watɨ.]

I need to go to the restroom.

Мені треба в туалет.
[mɛ'ni 'trɛba w tua'lɛt.]

I have to go.

Мені вже час.
[mɛ'ni wʒɛ tʃas.]

I have to go now.

Мушу вже йти.
['muʃu wʒɛ jtɨ.]

Asking for directions

Excuse me, …	**Вибачте, …** ['wɨbatʃtɛ, …]
Where is …?	**Де знаходиться …?** [dɛ zna'hɔdɨtʲsʲa …?]
Which way is …?	**В якому напрямку знаходиться …?** [w ja'kɔmu 'naprʲamku zna'hɔdɨtʲsʲa …?]
Could you help me, please?	**Допоможіть мені, будь ласка.** [dopomo'ʒitʲ mɛ'ni, budʲ 'laska.]

I'm looking for …	**Я шукаю …** [ja ʃu'kaʲu …]
I'm looking for the exit.	**Я шукаю вихід.** [ja ʃu'kaʲu 'wɨhid.]

I'm going to …	**Я їду в …** [ja 'idu w …]
Am I going the right way to …?	**Чи правильно я йду …?** [tʃɨ 'prawɨlʲno ja jdu …?]

Is it far?	**Це далеко?** [tsɛ da'lɛko?]
Can I get there on foot?	**Чи дійду я туди пішки?** [tʃɨ dij'du ja tu'dɨ 'piʃkɨ?]
Can you show me on the map?	**Покажіть мені на карті, будь ласка.** [poka'ʒitʲ mɛ'ni na 'karti, budʲ 'laska.]
Show me where we are right now.	**Покажіть, де ми зараз.** [poka'ʒitʲ, dɛ mɨ 'zaraz.]

Here	**Тут** [tut]
There	**Там** [tam]
This way	**Сюди** [sʲu'dɨ]

Turn right.	**Поверніть направо.** [powɛr'nitʲ na'prawo.]
Turn left.	**Поверніть наліво.** [powɛr'nitʲ na'liwo.]
first (second, third) turn	**перший (другий, третій) поворот** ['pɛrʃɨj ('druɦɨj, 'trɛtij) powo'rɔt]
to the right	**направо** [na'prawo]

to the left

налі́во
[na'liwo]

Go straight ahead.

Іді́ть пря́мо.
[i'ditʲ 'prʲamo.]

Signs

WELCOME!	ЛАСКАВО ПРОСИМО [las'kawo 'prɔsɨmo]
ENTRANCE	ВХІД [whid]
EXIT	ВИХІД ['wɨhid]

PUSH	ВІД СЕБЕ [wid 'sɛbɛ]
PULL	ДО СЕБЕ [do 'sɛbɛ]
OPEN	ВІДКРИТО [wid'krɨto]
CLOSED	ЗАКРИТО [za'krɨto]

FOR WOMEN	ДЛЯ ЖІНОК [dlʲa ʒi'nɔk]
FOR MEN	ДЛЯ ЧОЛОВІКІВ [dlʲa tʃolowi'kiw]
GENTLEMEN, GENTS (m)	ЧОЛОВІЧИЙ ТУАЛЕТ [tʃolo'witʃij tua'lɛt]
WOMEN (f)	ЖІНОЧИЙ ТУАЛЕТ [ʒi'nɔtʃij tua'lɛt]

DISCOUNTS	ЗНИЖКИ ['znɨʒkɨ]
SALE	РОЗПРОДАЖ [roz'prɔdaʒ]
FREE	БЕЗКОШТОВНО [bɛzkoʃ'towno]
NEW!	НОВИНКА! [no'wɨnka!]
ATTENTION!	УВАГА! [u'waɦa!]

NO VACANCIES	МІСЦЬ НЕМАЄ [mists nɛ'maɛ]
RESERVED	ЗАРЕЗЕРВОВАНО [zarɛzɛr'wowano]
ADMINISTRATION	АДМІНІСТРАЦІЯ [admini'stratsiʲa]
STAFF ONLY	ТІЛЬКИ ДЛЯ ПЕРСОНАЛУ ['tilʲkɨ dlʲa pɛrso'nalu]

BEWARE OF THE DOG!	**ЗЛИЙ СОБАКА** [zlij so'baka]
NO SMOKING!	**НЕ ПАЛИТИ!** [nɛ pa'lɨtɨ!]
DO NOT TOUCH!	**РУКАМИ НЕ ТОРКАТИСЯ!** [ru'kamɨ nɛ tor'katɨsʲa!]
DANGEROUS	**НЕБЕЗПЕЧНО** [nɛbɛz'pɛtʃno]
DANGER	**НЕБЕЗПЕКА** [nɛbɛz'pɛka]
HIGH VOLTAGE	**ВИСОКА НАПРУГА** [wɨ'sɔka na'pruɦa]
NO SWIMMING!	**КУПАТИСЯ ЗАБОРОНЕНО** [ku'patɨsʲa zabo'rɔnɛno]

OUT OF ORDER	**НЕ ПРАЦЮЄ** [nɛ pra'tsʲuɛ]
FLAMMABLE	**ВОГНЕНЕБЕЗПЕЧНО** ['woɦnɛ nɛbɛz'pɛtʃno]
FORBIDDEN	**ЗАБОРОНЕНО** [zabo'rɔnɛno]
NO TRESPASSING!	**ПРОХІД ЗАБОРОНЕНИЙ** [pro'hid zabo'rɔnɛnɨj]
WET PAINT	**ПОФАРБОВАНО** [pofar'bowano]

CLOSED FOR RENOVATIONS	**ЗАКРИТО НА РЕМОНТ** [za'krɨto na rɛ'mɔnt]
WORKS AHEAD	**РЕМОНТНІ РОБОТИ** [rɛ'mɔntni ro'bɔtɨ]
DETOUR	**ОБ'ЇЗД** [ob"izd]

Transportation. General phrases

plane	**літак** [li'tak]
train	**поїзд** ['pɔizd]
bus	**автобус** [aw'tɔbus]
ferry	**пором** [po'rɔm]
taxi	**таксі** [tak'si]
car	**автомобіль** [awtomo'bilʲ]
schedule	**розклад** ['rɔzklad]
Where can I see the schedule?	**Де можна подивитися розклад?** [dɛ 'mɔʒna podi'witisʲa 'rɔzklad?]
workdays (weekdays)	**робочі дні** [ro'bɔʧi dni]
weekends	**вихідні дні** [wɨhid'ni dni]
holidays	**святкові дні** [swʲat'kɔwi dni]
DEPARTURE	**ВІДПРАВЛЕННЯ** [wid'prawlɛnʲa]
ARRIVAL	**ПРИБУТТЯ** [prɨbut'tʲa]
DELAYED	**ЗАТРИМУЄТЬСЯ** [za'trɨmuɛtʲsʲa]
CANCELLED	**ВІДМІНЕНИЙ** [wid'minɛnɨj]
next (train, etc.)	**наступний** [na'stupnɨj]
first	**перший** ['pɛrʃɨj]
last	**останній** [os'tanij]
When is the next ...?	**Коли буде наступний ...?** [ko'lɨ 'budɛ na'stupnɨj ...?]
When is the first ...?	**Коли відправляється перший ...?** [ko'lɨ widpraw'lʲaɛtʲsʲa 'pɛrʃɨj ...?]

When is the last ...?
Коли відправляється останній ...?
[koˈlɨ widprawˈlʲaɛtʲsʲa osˈtanij ...?]

transfer (change of trains, etc.)
пересадка
[pɛrɛˈsadka]

to make a transfer
зробити пересадку
[zroˈbɨtɨ pɛrɛˈsadku]

Do I need to make a transfer?
Чи потрібно мені робити пересадку?
[ʧɨ potˈribno mɛˈni roˈbɨtɨ pɛrɛˈsadku?]

Buying tickets

Where can I buy tickets?	**Де я можу купити квитки?** [dɛ ja 'mɔʒu ku'pɨtɨ kwɨt'kɨ?]
ticket	**квиток** [kwɨ'tɔk]
to buy a ticket	**купити квиток** [ku'pɨtɨ kwɨ'tɔk]
ticket price	**вартість квитка** ['wartistʲ kwɨt'ka]
Where to?	**Куди?** [ku'dɨ?]
To what station?	**До якої станції?** [do ja'kɔi 'stantsii?]
I need …	**Мені потрібно …** [mɛ'ni po'tribno …]
one ticket	**один квиток** [o'dɨn kwɨ'tɔk]
two tickets	**два квитки** [dwa kwɨt'kɨ]
three tickets	**три квитки** [trɨ kwɨt'kɨ]
one-way	**в один кінець** [w o'dɨn ki'nɛts]
round-trip	**туди і назад** [tu'dɨ i na'zad]
first class	**перший клас** ['pɛrʃɨj klas]
second class	**другий клас** ['druɦɨj klas]
today	**сьогодні** [sʲo'ɦɔdni]
tomorrow	**завтра** ['zawtra]
the day after tomorrow	**післязавтра** [pislʲa'zawtra]
in the morning	**вранці** ['wrantsi]
in the afternoon	**вдень** ['wdɛnʲ]
in the evening	**ввечері** ['wvɛtʃɛri]

aisle seat	**місце біля проходу** ['mistsɛ 'bilʲa pro'hɔdu]
window seat	**місце біля вікна** ['mistsɛ 'bilʲa wik'na]
How much?	**Скільки?** ['skilʲki?]
Can I pay by credit card?	**Чи можу я заплатити карткою?** [ʧi 'mɔʒu ja zapla'titi 'kartkoʲu?]

Bus

bus	**автобус** [awˈtɔbus]
intercity bus	**міжміський автобус** [miʒmisʲˈkij awˈtɔbus]
bus stop	**автобусна зупинка** [awˈtɔbusna zuˈpɨnka]
Where's the nearest bus stop?	**Де найближча автобусна зупинка?** [dɛ najbˈlɨʒtʃa awˈtɔbusna zuˈpɨnka?]
number (bus ~, etc.)	**номер** [ˈnɔmɛr]
Which bus do I take to get to …?	**Який автобус їде до …?** [jaˈkɨj awˈtɔbus ˈidɛ do …?]
Does this bus go to …?	**Цей автобус їде до …?** [tsɛj awˈtɔbus ˈidɛ do …?]
How frequent are the buses?	**Як часто ходять автобуси?** [jak ˈtʃasto ˈhɔdʲatʲ awˈtɔbusɨ?]
every 15 minutes	**кожні 15 хвилин** [ˈkɔʒni pʲjatˈnadtsʲatʲ hwɨˈlɨn]
every half hour	**щопівгодини** [ɕopiwɦoˈdɨnɨ]
every hour	**щогодини** [ɕoɦoˈdɨnɨ]
several times a day	**кілька разів на день** [ˈkilʲka raˈziw na dɛnʲ]
… times a day	**… разів на день** [… raˈziw na ˈdɛnʲ]
schedule	**розклад** [ˈrɔzklad]
Where can I see the schedule?	**Де можна подивитися розклад?** [dɛ ˈmɔʒna podɨˈwɨtɨsʲa ˈrɔzklad?]
When is the next bus?	**Коли буде наступний автобус?** [koˈlɨ ˈbudɛ naˈstupnɨj awˈtɔbus?]
When is the first bus?	**Коли відправляється перший автобус?** [koˈlɨ widprawˈlʲaɛtʲsʲa ˈpɛrʃɨj awˈtɔbus?]
When is the last bus?	**Коли їде останній автобус?** [koˈlɨ ˈidɛ osˈtanij awˈtɔbus?]

stop

next stop

last stop (terminus)

Stop here, please.

Excuse me, this is my stop.

зупинка
[zu'pɨnka]

наступна зупинка
[na'stupna zu'pɨnka]

кінцева зупинка
[kin'tsɛwa zu'pɨnka]

Зупиніть тут, будь ласка.
[zupɨ'nitʲ tut, budʲ 'laska.]

Дозвольте, це моя зупинка.
[doz'wolʲtɛ, tsɛ mo'ʲa zu'pɨnka.]

Train

train	**поїзд** ['pɔizd]
suburban train	**приміський поїзд** [priˈmisʲˈkij 'pɔizd]
long-distance train	**поїзд далекого прямування** ['pɔizd da'lɛkoɦo prʲamu'wanʲa]
train station	**вокзал** [wokˈzal]
Excuse me, where is the exit to the platform?	**Вибачте, де вихід до поїздів?** ['wibatʃtɛ, dɛ 'wihid do poiz'diw?]

Does this train go to ...?	**Цей поїзд їде до ...?** [tsɛj 'pɔizd 'idɛ do ...?]
next train	**наступний поїзд** [naˈstupnij 'pɔizd]
When is the next train?	**Коли буде наступний поїзд?** [ko'li 'budɛ na'stupnij 'pɔizd?]
Where can I see the schedule?	**Де можна подивитися розклад?** [dɛ 'mɔʒna podi'witisʲa 'rɔzklad?]
From which platform?	**З якої платформи?** [z ja'kɔi plat'fɔrmi?]
When does the train arrive in ...?	**Коли поїзд прибуває в ...?** [ko'li 'pɔizd pribu'waɛ w ...?]

Please help me.	**Допоможіть мені, будь ласка.** [dopomo'ʒitʲ mɛ'ni, budʲ 'laska.]
I'm looking for my seat.	**Я шукаю своє місце.** [ja ʃu'kaʲu swo'ɛ 'mistsɛ.]
We're looking for our seats.	**Ми шукаємо наші місця.** [mi ʃu'kaɛmo 'naʃi mis'tsʲa.]
My seat is taken.	**Моє місце зайняте.** [mo'ɛ 'mistsɛ 'zajnʲatɛ.]
Our seats are taken.	**Наші місця зайняті.** ['naʃi mis'tsʲa 'zajnʲati.]

I'm sorry but this is my seat.	**Вибачте, будь ласка, але це моє місце.** ['wibatʃtɛ, budʲ 'laska, a'lɛ tsɛ mo'ɛ 'mistsɛ.]
Is this seat taken?	**Це місце вільне?** [tsɛ 'mistsɛ 'wilʲnɛ?]
May I sit here?	**Можна мені тут сісти?** ['mɔʒna mɛ'ni tut 'sisti?]

On the train. Dialogue (No ticket)

Ticket, please.
Ваш квиток, будь ласка.
[waʃ kwɨ'tɔk, budʲ 'laska.]

I don't have a ticket.
У мене немає квитка.
[u 'mɛnɛ nɛ'maɛ kwɨt'ka.]

I lost my ticket.
Я загубив /загубила/ свій квиток.
[ja zaɦu'bɨw /zaɦu'bɨla/ swij kwɨ'tɔk.]

I forgot my ticket at home.
Я забув /забула/ квиток вдома.
[ja za'buw /za'bula/ kwɨ'tɔk 'wdoma.]

You can buy a ticket from me.
Ви можете купити квиток у мене.
[wɨ 'mɔʒɛtɛ ku'pɨtɨ kwɨ'tɔk u 'mɛnɛ.]

You will also have to pay a fine.
Вам ще доведеться заплатити штраф.
[wam ɕɛ dowɛ'dɛtʲsʲa zapla'tɨtɨ ʃtraf.]

Okay.
Добре.
['dobrɛ.]

Where are you going?
Куди ви їдете?
[ku'dɨ wɨ 'idɛtɛ?]

I'm going to ...
Я їду до ...
[ja 'idu do ...]

How much? I don't understand.
Скільки? Я не розумію.
['skilʲkɨ? ja nɛ rozu'miʲu.]

Write it down, please.
Напишіть, будь ласка.
[napɨ'ʃitʲ, budʲ 'laska.]

Okay. Can I pay with a credit card?
Добре. Чи можу я заплатити карткою?
['dobrɛ. ʧɨ 'mɔʒu ja zapla'tɨtɨ 'kartkoʲu?]

Yes, you can.
Так, можете.
[tak, 'mɔʒɛtɛ.]

Here's your receipt.
Ось ваша квитанція.
[osʲ 'waʃa kwɨ'tantsiʲa.]

Sorry about the fine.
Шкодую про штраф.
[ʃko'duʲu pro 'ʃtraf.]

That's okay. It was my fault.
Це нічого. Це моя вина.
[ʦɛ ni'ʧoɦo ʦɛ mo'ʲa wɨ'na.]

Enjoy your trip.
Приємної вам поїздки.
[prɨ'ɛmnoi wam po'izdkɨ.]

Taxi

taxi	**таксі** [tak'si]
taxi driver	**таксист** [tak'sist]
to catch a taxi	**зловити таксі** [zlo'witi tak'si]
taxi stand	**стоянка таксі** [sto'ʲanka tak'si]
Where can I get a taxi?	**Де я можу взяти таксі?** [dɛ ja 'mɔʒu 'wzʲati tak'si?]
to call a taxi	**викликати таксі** ['wiklikati tak'si]
I need a taxi.	**Мені потрібно таксі.** [mɛ'ni po'tribno tak'si.]
Right now.	**Просто зараз.** ['prɔsto 'zaraz.]
What is your address (location)?	**Ваша адреса?** ['waʃa ad'rɛsa?]
My address is …	**Моя адреса …** [mo'ʲa ad'rɛsa …]
Your destination?	**Куди ви поїдете?** [ku'di wi po'idɛtɛ?]
Excuse me, …	**Вибачте, …** ['wibatʃtɛ, …]
Are you available?	**Ви вільні?** [wi 'wilʲni?]
How much is it to get to …?	**Скільки коштує доїхати до …?** ['skilʲki 'kɔʃtuɛ do'ihati do …?]
Do you know where it is?	**Ви знаєте, де це?** [wi 'znaɛtɛ, dɛ tsɛ?]
Airport, please.	**В аеропорт, будь ласка.** [w aɛro'pɔrt, budʲ 'laska.]
Stop here, please.	**Зупиніться тут, будь ласка.** [zupi'nitʲsʲa tut, budʲ 'laska.]
It's not here.	**Це не тут.** [tsɛ nɛ tut.]
This is the wrong address.	**Це неправильна адреса.** [tsɛ nɛ'prawilʲna ad'rɛsa.]
Turn left.	**Зараз наліво.** ['zaraz na'liwo.]

Turn right.	**Зараз направо.** ['zaraz na'prawo.]
How much do I owe you?	**Скільки я вам винен /винна/?** ['skilʲkɨ ja wam 'wɨnɛn /'wɨna/?]
I'd like a receipt, please.	**Дайте мені чек, будь ласка.** ['dajtɛ mɛ'ni ʧɛk, budʲ 'laska.]
Keep the change.	**Здачі не треба.** ['zdaʧi nɛ 'trɛba.]

Would you please wait for me?	**Зачекайте мене, будь ласка.** [zaʧɛ'kajtɛ mɛ'nɛ, budʲ 'laska.]
five minutes	**5 хвилин** ['pʲatʲ hwɨ'lɨn]
ten minutes	**10 хвилин** ['dɛsʲatʲ hwɨ'lɨn]
fifteen minutes	**15 хвилин** [pʲat'nadtsʲatʲ hwɨ'lɨn]
twenty minutes	**20 хвилин** ['dwadtsʲatʲ hwɨ'lɨn]
half an hour	**півгодини** [piwɦo'dɨnɨ]

Hotel

Hello.
Добрий день.
['dɔbrij dɛnʲ.]

My name is …
Мене звуть …
[mɛ'nɛ zwutʲ …]

I have a reservation.
Я резервував /резервувала/ номер.
[ja rɛzɛrwu'waw /rɛzɛrwu'wala/ 'nɔmɛr.]

I need …
Мені потрібен …
[mɛ'ni po'tribɛn …]

a single room
одномісний номер
[odno'misnij 'nɔmɛr]

a double room
двомісний номер
[dwo'misnij 'nɔmɛr]

How much is that?
Скільки він коштує?
['skilʲki win 'kɔʃtuɛ?]

That's a bit expensive.
Це трохи дорого.
[ʦɛ 'trɔhi 'dɔroho.]

Do you have anything else?
У вас є ще що-небудь?
[u was 'ɛ ɕɛ ɕo-'nɛbudʲ?]

I'll take it.
Я візьму його.
[ja wizʲ'mu ʲo'hɔ.]

I'll pay in cash.
Я заплачу готівкою.
[ja zapla'ʧu ɦo'tiwkoʲu.]

I've got a problem.
У мене є проблема.
[u 'mɛnɛ ɛ prob'lɛma.]

My … is out of order.
У мене не працює …
[u 'mɛnɛ nɛ pra'ʦʲuɛ …]

TV
телевізор
[tɛlɛ'wizor]

air conditioner
кондиціонер
[kondiʦio'nɛr]

tap
кран
[kran]

shower
душ
[duʃ]

sink
раковина
['rakowina]

safe
сейф
[sɛjf]

door lock
замок
[za'mɔk]

electrical outlet	**розетка** [ro'zɛtka]
hairdryer	**фен** [fɛn]

I don't have …	**У мене немає …** [u 'mɛnɛ nɛ'maɛ …]
water	**води** [wo'dɨ]
light	**світла** ['switla]
electricity	**електрики** [ɛ'lɛktrɨkɨ]

Can you give me …?	**Чи не можете мені дати …?** [tʃɨ nɛ 'mɔʒɛtɛ mɛ'ni 'datɨ …?]
a towel	**рушник** [ruʃ'nɨk]
a blanket	**ковдру** ['kɔwdru]
slippers	**тапочки** ['tapotʃkɨ]
a robe	**халат** [ha'lat]
shampoo	**шампунь** [ʃam'punʲ]
soap	**мило** ['mɨlo]

I'd like to change rooms.	**Я б хотів /хотіла/ поміняти номер.** [ja b ho'tiw /ho'tila/ pomi'nʲatɨ 'nɔmɛr.]
I can't find my key.	**Я не можу знайти свій ключ.** [ja nɛ 'mɔʒu znaj'tɨ swij 'klʲutʃ.]
Could you open my room, please?	**Відкрийте мій номер, будь ласка.** [wid'krijtɛ mij 'nɔmɛr, budʲ 'laska.]
Who's there?	**Хто там?** [hto tam?]
Come in!	**Заходьте!** [za'hɔdʲtɛ!]
Just a minute!	**Одну хвилину!** [od'nu hwɨ'lɨnu!]
Not right now, please.	**Будь ласка, не зараз.** [budʲ 'laska, nɛ 'zaraz.]

Come to my room, please.	**Зайдіть до мене, будь ласка.** [zaj'ditʲ do 'mɛnɛ, budʲ 'laska.]
I'd like to order food service.	**Я хочу зробити замовлення їжі в номер.** [ja 'hɔtʃu zro'bɨtɨ za'mɔwlɛnja 'iʒi w 'nɔmɛr.]
My room number is …	**Мій номер кімнати …** [mij 'nɔmɛr kim'natɨ …]

I'm leaving …	**Я їду …** [ja 'idu …]
We're leaving …	**Ми їдемо …** [mɨ 'idɛmo …]
right now	**зараз** ['zaraz]
this afternoon	**сьогодні після обіду** [sʲo'ɦɔdni 'pislʲa o'bidu]
tonight	**сьогодні ввечері** [sʲo'ɦɔdni 'wvɛʧɛri]
tomorrow	**завтра** ['zawtra]
tomorrow morning	**завтра вранці** ['zawtra 'wrantsi]
tomorrow evening	**завтра ввечері** ['zawtra 'wvɛʧɛri]
the day after tomorrow	**післязавтра** [pislʲa'zawtra]

I'd like to pay.	**Я б хотів /хотіла/ розрахуватися.** [ja b ho'tiw /ho'tila/ rozrahu'watisʲa.]
Everything was wonderful.	**Все було чудово.** [wsɛ bu'lɔ ʧu'dɔwo.]
Where can I get a taxi?	**Де я можу взяти таксі?** [dɛ ja 'mɔʒu 'wzʲatɨ tak'si?]
Would you call a taxi for me, please?	**Викличте мені таксі, будь ласка.** ['wɨklɨʧtɛ mɛ'ni tak'si, budʲ 'laska.]

Restaurant

Can I look at the menu, please?
Чи можу я подивитися ваше меню?
[tʃɨ 'mɔʒu ja podɨ'witisʲa 'waʃɛ mɛ'nʲu?]

Table for one.
Столик для одного.
['stɔlɨk dlʲa od'nɔɦo.]

There are two (three, four) of us.
Нас двоє (троє, четверо).
[nas 'dwɔɛ ('trɔɛ, 'tʃɛtwɛro).]

Smoking
Для курців
[dlʲa kur'tsiw]

No smoking
Для некурців
[dlʲa nɛkur'tsiw]

Excuse me! (addressing a waiter)
Будьте ласкаві!
['budʲtɛ las'kawi!]

menu
меню
[mɛ'nʲu]

wine list
карта вин
['karta wɨn]

The menu, please.
Меню, будь ласка.
[mɛ'nʲu, budʲ 'laska.]

Are you ready to order?
Ви готові зробити замовлення?
[wɨ ɦo'tɔwi zro'bɨtɨ za'mɔwlɛnʲa?]

What will you have?
Що ви будете замовляти?
[ɕo wɨ 'budɛtɛ zamow'lʲatɨ?]

I'll have ...
Я буду ...
[ja 'budu ...]

I'm a vegetarian.
Я вегетаріанець /вегетаріанка/.
[ja wɛɦɛtari'anɛts /wɛɦɛtari'anka/.]

meat
м'ясо
['mʲaso]

fish
риба
['rɨba]

vegetables
овочі
['ɔwotʃi]

Do you have vegetarian dishes?
У вас є вегетаріанські страви?
[u was 'ɛ wɛɦɛtari'ansʲki 'strawɨ?]

I don't eat pork.
Я не їм свинину.
[ja nɛ im swɨ'nɨnu.]

He /she/ doesn't eat meat.
Він /вона/ не їсть м'ясо.
[win /wo'na/ nɛ istʲ 'mʲaso.]

I am allergic to ...
У мене алергія на ...
[u 'mɛnɛ alɛr'ɦiʲa na ...]

Would you please bring me …

Принесіть мені, будь ласка …
[prinɛ'sitʲ mɛ'ni, budʲ 'laska …]

salt | pepper | sugar

сіль | перець | цукор
[silʲ | 'pɛrɛts | 'tsukor]

coffee | tea | dessert

каву | чай | десерт
['kawu | tʃaj | dɛ'sɛrt]

water | sparkling | plain

воду | з газом | без газу
['wɔdu | z 'ɦazom | bɛz 'ɦazu]

a spoon | fork | knife

ложку | вилку | ніж
['lɔʒku | 'wɪłku | niʒ]

a plate | napkin

тарілку | серветку
[ta'riłku | sɛr'wɛtku]

Enjoy your meal!

Смачного!
[smatʃ'nɔɦo!]

One more, please.

Принесіть ще, будь ласка.
[prinɛ'sitʲ ɕɛ, budʲ 'laska.]

It was very delicious.

Було дуже смачно.
[bu'lɔ 'duʒɛ 'smatʃno.]

---

check | change | tip

рахунок | здача | чайові
[ra'ɦunok | 'zdatʃa | tʃaɪo'wi]

Check, please.
(Could I have the check, please?)

Рахунок, будь ласка.
[ra'ɦunok, budʲ 'laska.]

Can I pay by credit card?

Чи можу я заплатити карткою?
[tʃi 'mɔʒu ja zapla'tɪtʲi 'kartkoʲu?]

I'm sorry, there's a mistake here.

Вибачте, тут помилка.
['wɪbatʃtɛ, tut po'mɪłka.]

Shopping

Can I help you?
Чи можу я вам допомогти?
[tʃɨ 'mɔʒu ja wam dopomoɦ'tɨ?]

Do you have ...?
У вас є ...?
[u was 'ɛ ...?]

I'm looking for ...
Я шукаю ...
[ja ʃu'kaʲu ...]

I need ...
Мені потрібен ...
[mɛ'ni po'tribɛn ...]

I'm just looking.
Я просто дивлюся.
[ja 'prɔsto 'dɨwlʲusʲa.]

We're just looking.
Ми просто дивимося.
[mɨ 'prɔsto 'dɨwɨmosʲa.]

I'll come back later.
Я зайду пізніше.
[ja zaj'du piz'niʃɛ.]

We'll come back later.
Ми зайдемо пізніше.
[mɨ 'zajdɛmo piz'niʃɛ.]

discounts | sale
знижки | розпродаж
['znɨʒkɨ | roz'prɔdaʒ]

Would you please show me ...
Покажіть мені, будь ласка ...
[poka'ʒitʲ mɛ'ni, budʲ 'laska ...]

Would you please give me ...
Дайте мені, будь ласка ...
['dajtɛ mɛ'ni, budʲ 'laska ...]

Can I try it on?
Чи можна мені це приміряти?
[tʃɨ 'mɔʒna mɛ'ni tsɛ prɨ'mirʲatɨ?]

Excuse me, where's the fitting room?
Вибачте, де примірювальна?
['wɨbatʃtɛ, dɛ prɨ'mirʲuwalʲna?]

Which color would you like?
Який колір ви хочете?
[ja'kɨj 'kolir wɨ 'hɔtʃɛtɛ?]

size | length
розмір | зріст
['rozmir | zrist]

How does it fit?
Підійшло?
[pidij'ʃlɔ?]

How much is it?
Скільки це коштує?
['skilʲkɨ tsɛ 'koʃtuɛ?]

That's too expensive.
Це занадто дорого.
[tsɛ za'nadto 'dɔroɦo.]

I'll take it.
Я візьму це.
[ja wizʲ'mu tsɛ.]

Excuse me, where do I pay?
Вибачте, де каса?
['wɨbatʃtɛ, dɛ 'kasa?]

| Will you pay in cash or credit card? | **Як ви будете платити? Готівкою чи кредиткою?**
[jak wɨ 'budɛtɛ pla'tɨtɨ? ɦo'tiwkoʲu ʧɨ krɛ'dɨtkoʲu?] |
| In cash | with credit card | **готівкою | карткою**
[ɦo'tiwkoʲu | 'kartkoʲu] |

Do you want the receipt?	**Вам потрібен чек?** [wam po'tribɛn ʧɛk?]
Yes, please.	**Так, будьте ласкаві.** [tak, 'budʲtɛ las'kawi.]
No, it's OK.	**Ні, не потрібно. Дякую.** [ni, nɛ po'tribno. 'dʲakuʲu.]
Thank you. Have a nice day!	**Дякую. На все добре!** ['dʲakuʲu. na wsɛ 'dɔbrɛ.]

In town

Excuse me, please.	**Вибачте, будь ласка …** ['wɨbatʃtɛ, budʲ 'laska …]
I'm looking for …	**Я шукаю …** [ja ʃu'kaʲu …]
the subway	**метро** [mɛt'rɔ]
my hotel	**свій готель** [swij ɦo'tɛlʲ]
the movie theater	**кінотеатр** [kinotɛ'atr]
a taxi stand	**стоянку таксі** [sto'ʲanku tak'si]
an ATM	**банкомат** [banko'mat]
a foreign exchange office	**обмін валют** ['ɔbmin wa'lʲut]
an internet café	**інтернет-кафе** [intɛr'nɛt-ka'fɛ]
… street	**вулицю …** ['wulɨtsʲu …]
this place	**ось це місце** [osʲ tsɛ 'mistsɛ]
Do you know where … is?	**Чи не знаєте Ви, де знаходиться …?** [tʃɨ nɛ 'znaɛtɛ wɨ, dɛ zna'ɦodɨtsʲa …?]
Which street is this?	**Як називається ця вулиця?** [jak nazɨ'waɛtsʲa tsʲa 'wulɨtsʲa?]
Show me where we are right now.	**Покажіть, де ми зараз.** [poka'ʒitʲ, dɛ mɨ 'zaraz.]
Can I get there on foot?	**Я дійду туди пішки?** [ja dij'du tu'dɨ 'piʃkɨ?]
Do you have a map of the city?	**У вас є карта міста?** [u was 'ɛ 'karta 'mista?]
How much is a ticket to get in?	**Скільки коштує вхідний квиток?** ['skilʲkɨ 'koʃtuɛ whid'nij kwɨ'tɔk?]
Can I take pictures here?	**Чи можна тут фотографувати?** [tʃɨ 'moʒna tut fotoɦrafu'watɨ?]
Are you open?	**Ви відкриті?** [wɨ widk'rɨti?]

When do you open?

О котрій ви відкриваєтесь?
[o kot'rij wɨ widkrɨ'waɛtɛsʲ?]

When do you close?

До котрої години ви працюєте?
[do ko'trɔi ɦo'dɨnɨ wɨ pra'ʦʲuɛtɛ?]

Money

money	**гроші** ['ɦrɔʃi]
cash	**готівкові гроші** [ɦotiw'kɔwi 'ɦrɔʃi]
paper money	**паперові гроші** [papɛ'rɔwi 'ɦrɔʃi]
loose change	**дрібні гроші** [drib'ni 'ɦrɔʃi]
check | change | tip	**рахунок | здача | чайові** [ra'ɦunok | 'zdatʃa | tʃaʲo'wi]

credit card	**кредитна картка** [krɛ'ditna 'kartka]
wallet	**гаманець** [ɦama'nɛts]
to buy	**купувати** [kupu'wati]
to pay	**платити** [pla'titi]
fine	**штраф** ['ʃtraf]
free	**безкоштовно** [bɛzkoʃ'tɔwno]

Where can I buy …?	**Де я можу купити …?** [dɛ ja 'mɔʒu ku'piti …?]
Is the bank open now?	**Чи відкритий зараз банк?** [tʃi wid'kritij 'zaraz bank?]
When does it open?	**О котрій він відкривається?** [o kot'rij win widkri'waɛtʲsʲa?]
When does it close?	**До котрої години він працює?** [do ko'trɔi ɦo'dini win pra'tsʲuɛ?]

How much?	**Скільки?** ['skilʲki?]
How much is this?	**Скільки це коштує?** ['skilʲki tsɛ 'kɔʃtuɛ?]
That's too expensive.	**Це занадто дорого.** [tsɛ za'nadto 'dɔrоɦo.]

Excuse me, where do I pay?	**Вибачте, де каса?** ['wibatʃtɛ, dɛ 'kasa?]
Check, please.	**Рахунок, будь ласка.** [ra'ɦunok, budʲ 'laska.]

Can I pay by credit card? | **Чи можу я заплатити карткою?**
[ʧɨ 'mɔʒu ja zapla'tɨtɨ 'kartkoʲu?]

Is there an ATM here? | **Тут є банкомат?**
[tut ɛ banko'mat?]

I'm looking for an ATM. | **Мені потрібен банкомат.**
[mɛ'ni po'tribɛn banko'mat.]

I'm looking for a foreign exchange office. | **Я шукаю обмін валют.**
[ja ʃu'kaʲu 'ɔbmin wa'lʲut.]

I'd like to change … | **Я б хотів /хотіла/ поміняти …**
[ja b ho'tiw /ho'tila/ pomi'nʲatɨ …]

What is the exchange rate? | **Який курс обміну?**
[ja'kɨj kurs 'ɔbminu?]

Do you need my passport? | **Вам потрібен мій паспорт?**
[wam po'tribɛn mij 'pasport?]

Time

What time is it?	**Котра година?** [ko'tra ɦo'dɨna?]
When?	**Коли?** [ko'lɨ?]
At what time?	**О котрій?** [o kot'rij?]
now | later | after …	**зараз | пізніше | після …** ['zaraz | piz'niʃɛ | 'pislʲa …]
one o'clock	**перша година дня** ['pɛrʃa ɦo'dɨna dnʲa]
one fifteen	**п'ятнадцять на другу** [pʲat'nadʦʲatʲ na 'druɦu]
one thirty	**половина другої** [polo'wɨna 'druɦoi]
one forty-five	**за п'ятнадцять друга** [za pʲat'natʦʲatʲ 'druɦa]
one | two | three	**один | два | три** [o'dɨn | dwa | trɨ]
four | five | six	**чотири | п'ять | шість** [ʧo'tɨrɨ | 'pʲatʲ | ʃistʲ]
seven | eight | nine	**сім | вісім | дев'ять** [sim | 'wisim | 'dɛwʲatʲ]
ten | eleven | twelve	**десять | одинадцять | дванадцять** ['dɛsʲatʲ | odɨ'nadʦʲatʲ | dwa'nadʦʲatʲ]
in …	**через …** ['ʧɛrɛz …]
five minutes	**5 хвилин** ['pʲatʲ hwɨ'lɨn]
ten minutes	**10 хвилин** ['dɛsʲatʲ hwɨ'lɨn]
fifteen minutes	**15 хвилин** [pʲat'nadʦʲatʲ hwɨ'lɨn]
twenty minutes	**20 хвилин** ['dwadʦʲatʲ hwɨ'lɨn]
half an hour	**півгодини** [piwɦo'dɨnɨ]
an hour	**одна година** [od'na ɦo'dɨna]
in the morning	**вранці** ['wranʦi]
early in the morning	**рано вранці** ['rano 'wranʦi]

this morning	**сьогодні вранці** [sʲoˈɦɔdni ˈwrantsi]
tomorrow morning	**завтра вранці** [ˈzawtra ˈwrantsi]

in the middle of the day	**в обід** [w oˈbid]
in the afternoon	**після обіду** [ˈpislʲa oˈbidu]
in the evening	**ввечері** [ˈwvɛtʃɛri]
tonight	**сьогодні ввечері** [sʲoˈɦɔdni ˈwvɛtʃɛri]

at night	**вночі** [wnoˈtʃi]
yesterday	**вчора** [ˈwtʃora]
today	**сьогодні** [sʲoˈɦɔdni]
tomorrow	**завтра** [ˈzawtra]
the day after tomorrow	**післязавтра** [pislʲaˈzawtra]

What day is it today?	**Який сьогодні день?** [jaˈkij sʲoˈɦɔdni dɛnʲ?]
It's …	**Сьогодні …** [sʲoˈɦɔdni …]
Monday	**понеділок** [ponɛˈdilok]
Tuesday	**вівторок** [wiwˈtɔrok]
Wednesday	**середа** [sɛrɛˈda]

Thursday	**четвер** [tʃɛtˈwɛr]
Friday	**п'ятниця** [ˈpʲatnɨtsʲa]
Saturday	**субота** [suˈbota]
Sunday	**неділя** [nɛˈdilʲa]

Greetings. Introductions

Hello.	**Добрий день.** ['dɔbrɨj dɛnʲ.]
Pleased to meet you.	**Радий /рада/ з вами познайомитися.** ['radɨj /'rada/ z 'wamɨ pozna'jɔmɨtɨsʲa.]
Me too.	**Я теж.** [ja tɛʒ.]
I'd like you to meet …	**Знайомтеся. Це …** [zna'jɔmtɛsʲa. tsɛ …]
Nice to meet you.	**Дуже приємно.** ['duʒɛ prɨ'ɛmno.]

How are you?	**Як ви? Як у вас справи?** [jak wɨ? jak u was 'sprawɨ?]
My name is …	**Мене звуть …** [mɛ'nɛ zwutʲ …]
His name is …	**Його звуть …** [ʲo'ɦɔ zwutʲ …]
Her name is …	**Її звуть …** [ɨ̈ 'zwutʲ …]

What's your name?	**Як вас звуть?** [jak was 'zwutʲ?]
What's his name?	**Як його звуть?** [jak ʲo'ɦɔ zwutʲ?]
What's her name?	**Як її звуть?** [jak ɨ̈ 'zwutʲ?]

What's your last name?	**Яке ваше прізвище?** [ja'kɛ 'waʃɛ 'prizwɨɕɛ?]
You can call me …	**Називайте мене …** [nazɨ'wajtɛ mɛ'nɛ …]
Where are you from?	**Звідки ви?** ['zwidkɨ wɨ?]
I'm from …	**Я з …** [ja z …]
What do you do for a living?	**Ким ви працюєте?** [kɨm wɨ pra'tsʲuɛtɛ?]

Who is this?	**Хто це?** [hto tsɛ?]
Who is he?	**Хто він?** [hto win?]
Who is she?	**Хто вона?** [hto wo'na?]

Who are they?	**Хто вони?** [hto wo'nɨ?]
This is ...	**Це ...** [ʦɛ ...]
my friend (masc.)	**мій друг** [mij druɦ]
my friend (fem.)	**моя подруга** [mo'ʲa 'pɔdruɦa]
my husband	**мій чоловік** [mij ʧolo'wik]
my wife	**моя дружина** [mo'ʲa dru'ʒɨna]

my father	**мій батько** [mij 'batʲko]
my mother	**моя мама** [mo'ʲa 'mama]
my brother	**мій брат** [mij brat]
my sister	**моя сестра** [mo'ʲa sɛst'ra]
my son	**мій син** [mij sɨn]
my daughter	**моя дочка** [mo'ʲa doʧ'ka]

This is our son.	**Це наш син.** [ʦɛ naʃ sɨn.]
This is our daughter.	**Це наша дочка.** [ʦɛ 'naʃa doʧ'ka.]
These are my children.	**Це мої діти.** [ʦɛ mo'i 'ditɨ.]
These are our children.	**Це наші діти.** [ʦɛ 'naʃi 'ditɨ.]

Farewells

Good bye!
До побачення!
[do po'batʃɛnʲa!]

Bye! (inform.)
Бувай!
[bu'waj!]

See you tomorrow.
До завтра.
[do 'zawtra.]

See you soon.
До зустрічі.
[do 'zustritʃi.]

See you at seven.
Зустрінемось о сьомій.
[zust'rinɛmosʲ o 'sʲɔmij.]

Have fun!
Розважайтеся!
[rozwa'ʒajtɛsʲa!]

Talk to you later.
Поговоримо пізніше.
[poɦo'wɔrimo piz'niʃɛ.]

Have a nice weekend.
Вдалих вихідних.
['wdaɫih wihid'nih.]

Good night.
На добраніч.
[na do'braniʧ.]

It's time for me to go.
Мені вже час.
[mɛ'ni wʒɛ ʧas.]

I have to go.
Мушу йти.
['muʃu jtɨ.]

I will be right back.
Я зараз повернусь.
[ja 'zaraz powɛr'nusʲ.]

It's late.
Вже пізно.
[wʒɛ 'pizno.]

I have to get up early.
Мені рано вставати.
[mɛ'ni 'rano wsta'watɨ.]

I'm leaving tomorrow.
Я завтра від'їжджаю.
[ja 'zawtra widʔiʒ'dʒaʲu.]

We're leaving tomorrow.
Ми завтра від'їжджаємо.
[mɨ 'zawtra widʔiʒ'dʒaɛmo.]

Have a nice trip!
Щасливої поїздки!
[ɕas'ɫɨwoi po'izdkɨ!]

It was nice meeting you.
Було приємно з вами познайомитися.
[bu'ɫɔ prɨ'ɛmno z 'wamɨ pozna'jɔmɨtɨsʲa.]

It was nice talking to you.

Було приємно з вами поспілкуватися.
[bu'lɔ prɨ'ɛmno z 'wamɨ pospilku'watisʲa.]

Thanks for everything.

Дякую за все.
['dʲakuʲu za wsɛ.]

I had a very good time.

Я чудово провів /провела/ час.
[ja ʧu'dɔwo pro'wiw /prowɛ'la/ ʧas.]

We had a very good time.

Ми чудово провели час.
[mɨ ʧu'dɔwo prowɛ'lɨ ʧas.]

It was really great.

Все було чудово.
[wsɛ bu'lɔ ʧu'dɔwo.]

I'm going to miss you.

Я буду сумувати.
[ja 'budu sumu'watɨ.]

We're going to miss you.

Ми будемо сумувати.
[mɨ 'budɛmo sumu'watɨ.]

Good luck!

Успіхів! Щасливо!
['uspihiw! ɕas'lɨwo!]

Say hi to …

Передавайте вітання …
[pɛrɛda'wajtɛ wi'tanʲa …]

Foreign language

I don't understand.	**Я не розумію.** [ja nɛ rozu'miʲu.]
Write it down, please.	**Напишіть це, будь ласка.** [napiʲʃitʲ tsɛ, budʲ 'laska.]
Do you speak ...?	**Ви знаєте ...?** [wɨ 'znaɛtɛ ...?]

I speak a little bit of ...	**Я трохи знаю ...** [ja 'trɔhɨ znaʲu ...]
English	**англійська** [anɦ'lijsʲka]
Turkish	**турецька** [tu'rɛtska]
Arabic	**арабська** [a'rabsʲka]
French	**французька** [fran'tsuzʲka]

German	**німецька** [ni'mɛtska]
Italian	**італійська** [ita'lijsʲka]
Spanish	**іспанська** [is'pansʲka]
Portuguese	**португальська** [portu'ɦalʲsʲka]
Chinese	**китайська** [kɨ'tajsʲka]
Japanese	**японська** [ja'pɔnsʲka]

Can you repeat that, please.	**Повторіть, будь ласка.** [powto'ritʲ, budʲ 'laska.]
I understand.	**Я розумію.** [ja rozu'miʲu.]
I don't understand.	**Я не розумію.** [ja nɛ rozu'miʲu.]
Please speak more slowly.	**Говоріть повільніше, будь ласка.** [ɦowo'ritʲ po'wilʲniʃɛ, 'budʲ 'laska.]

| Is that correct? (Am I saying it right?) | **Це правильно?**
[tsɛ 'prawɨlʲno?] |
| What is this? (What does this mean?) | **Що це?**
[ɕo 'tsɛ?] |

Apologies

Excuse me, please.
Вибачте, будь ласка.
['wɨbatʃtɛ, budʲ 'laska.]

I'm sorry.
Мені шкода.
[mɛ'ni 'ʃkɔda.]

I'm really sorry.
Мені дуже шкода.
[mɛ'ni 'duʒɛ 'ʃkɔda.]

Sorry, it's my fault.
Винен /Винна/, це моя вина.
['wɨnɛn /'wɨna/ , ʦɛ mo'ʲa wɨ'na.]

My mistake.
Моя помилка.
[mo'ʲa po'mɨlka.]

May I ...?
Чи можу я ...?
[ʧɨ 'mɔʒu ja ...?]

Do you mind if I ...?
Ви не заперечуватимете, якщо я ...?
[wɨ nɛ zapɛ'rɛʧuwatɨmɛtɛ, jak'ɕɔ ja ...?]

It's OK.
Нічого страшного.
[ni'ʧɔho straʃ'nɔho.]

It's all right.
Все гаразд.
[wsɛ ɦa'razd.]

Don't worry about it.
Не турбуйтесь.
[nɛ tur'bujtɛsʲ.]

Agreement

Yes.	**Так.** [tak.]
Yes, sure.	**Так, звичайно.** [tak, zwɨ'tʃajno.]
OK (Good!)	**Добре!** ['dɔbrɛ!]
Very well.	**Дуже добре.** ['duʒɛ 'dɔbrɛ.]
Certainly!	**Звичайно!** [zwɨ'tʃajno!]
I agree.	**Я згідний /згідна/.** [ja 'zɦidnɨj /'zɦidna/.]

That's correct.	**Вірно.** ['wirno.]
That's right.	**Правильно.** ['prawɨlʲno.]
You're right.	**Ви праві.** [wɨ pra'wi.]
I don't mind.	**Я не заперечую.** [ja nɛ zapɛ'rɛtʃuˠu.]
Absolutely right.	**Абсолютно вірно.** [abso'lʲutno 'wirno.]

It's possible.	**Це можливо.** [tsɛ moʒ'lɨwo.]
That's a good idea.	**Це гарна думка.** [tsɛ 'ɦarna 'dumka.]
I can't say no.	**Не можу відмовити.** [nɛ 'mɔʒu wid'mɔwɨtɨ.]
I'd be happy to.	**Буду радий /рада/.** ['budu 'radɨj /'rada/.]
With pleasure.	**Із задоволенням.** [iz zado'wɔlɛnjam.]

Refusal. Expressing doubt

No.
Ні.
[ni.]

Certainly not.
Звичайно, ні.
[zwɨ'ʧajno, ni.]

I don't agree.
Я не згідний /згідна/.
[ja nɛ 'zɦidnɨj /'zɦidna/.]

I don't think so.
Я так не думаю.
[ja tak nɛ 'dumaʲu.]

It's not true.
Це неправда.
[ʦɛ nɛ'prawda.]

You are wrong.
Ви неправі.
[wɨ nɛpra'wi.]

I think you are wrong.
Я думаю, що ви неправі.
[ja 'dumaʲu, ɕo wɨ nɛpra'wi.]

I'm not sure.
Не впевнений /впевнена/.
[nɛ 'wpɛwnɛnɨj /'wpɛwnɛna/.]

It's impossible.
Це неможливо.
[ʦɛ nɛmoʒ'lɨwo.]

Nothing of the kind (sort)!
Нічого подібного!
[ni'ʧoɦo po'dibnoɦo!]

The exact opposite.
Навпаки!
[nawpa'kɨ!]

I'm against it.
Я проти.
[ja 'prɔtɨ.]

I don't care.
Мені все одно.
[mɛ'ni wsɛ od'nɔ.]

I have no idea.
Гадки не маю.
['ɦadkɨ nɛ 'maʲu.]

I doubt it.
Сумніваюся, що це так.
[sumni'waʲusʲa, ɕo ʦɛ tak.]

Sorry, I can't.
Вибачте, я не можу.
['wɨbaʧtɛ, ja nɛ 'mɔʒu.]

Sorry, I don't want to.
Вибачте, я не хочу.
['wɨbaʧtɛ, ja nɛ 'hɔʧu.]

Thank you, but I don't need this.
Дякую, мені це не потрібно.
['dʲakuʲu, mɛ'ni ʦɛ nɛ pot'ribno.]

It's getting late.
Вже пізно.
[wʒɛ 'pizno.]

I have to get up early.

Мені рано вставати.
[mɛˈni ˈrano wstaˈwatɨ.]

I don't feel well.

Я погано себе почуваю.
[ja poˈɦano sɛˈbɛ potʃuˈwaʲu.]

Expressing gratitude

Thank you.
Дякую.
['dʲakuʲu.]

Thank you very much.
Дуже дякую.
['duʒɛ 'dʲakuʲu.]

I really appreciate it.
Дуже вдячний /вдячна/.
['duʒɛ 'wdʲatʃnij /'wdʲatʃna/.]

I'm really grateful to you.
Я вам вдячний /вдячна/.
[ja wam 'wdʲatʃnij /'wdʲatʃna/.]

We are really grateful to you.
Ми Вам вдячні.
[mɨ wam 'wdʲatʃni.]

Thank you for your time.
Дякую, що витратили час.
['dʲakuʲu, ɕo 'wɨtratɨlɨ tʃas.]

Thanks for everything.
Дякую за все.
['dʲakuʲu za wsɛ.]

Thank you for ...
Дякую за ...
['dʲakuʲu za ...]

your help
вашу допомогу
['waʃu dopo'mɔɦu]

a nice time
гарний час
['ɦarnij tʃas]

a wonderful meal
чудову їжу
[tʃu'dɔwu 'iʒu]

a pleasant evening
приємний вечір
[prɨ'ɛmnij 'wɛtʃir]

a wonderful day
чудовий день
[tʃu'dɔwij dɛnʲ]

an amazing journey
цікаву екскурсію
[tsi'kawu ɛks'kursiʲu]

Don't mention it.
Нема за що.
[nɛ'ma za ɕo.]

You are welcome.
Не варто дякувати.
[nɛ 'warto 'dʲakuwatɨ.]

Any time.
Завжди будь ласка.
[za'wʒdɨ budʲ 'laska.]

My pleasure.
Був радий /Була рада/ допомогти.
[buw 'radij /bu'la 'rada/ dopomoɦ'tɨ.]

Forget it.
Забудьте. Все гаразд.
[za'budʲtɛ wsɛ ɦa'razd.]

Don't worry about it.
Не турбуйтесь.
[nɛ tur'bujtɛsʲ.]

Congratulations. Best wishes

Congratulations!	**Вітаю!** [wi'ta^ju!]
Happy birthday!	**З Днем народження!** [z dnɛm na'rɔdʒɛnʲa!]
Merry Christmas!	**Веселого Різдва!** [wɛ'sɛloɦo rizd'wa!]
Happy New Year!	**З Новим роком!** [z no'wɨm 'rɔkom!]
Happy Easter!	**Зі Світлим Великоднем!** [zi 'switlɨm wɛ'lɨkodnɛm!]
Happy Hanukkah!	**Щасливої Хануки!** [ɕas'lɨwoi ha'nuki!]
I'd like to propose a toast.	**У мене є тост.** [u 'mɛnɛ ɛ tost.]
Cheers!	**За ваше здоров'я!** [za 'waʃɛ zdo'rɔwʲa]
Let's drink to …!	**Вип'ємо за …!** ['wɨpʲɛmo za …!]
To our success!	**За наш успіх!** [za naʃ 'uspih!]
To your success!	**За ваш успіх!** [za waʃ 'uspih!]
Good luck!	**Успіхів!** ['uspihiw!]
Have a nice day!	**Гарного вам дня!** ['ɦarnoɦo wam dnʲa!]
Have a good holiday!	**Гарного вам відпочинку!** ['ɦarnoɦo wam widpo'tʃinku!]
Have a safe journey!	**Вдалої поїздки!** ['wdaloi po'izdki!]
I hope you get better soon!	**Бажаю вам швидкого одужання!** [ba'ʒa^ju wam ʃwɨd'kɔɦo o'duʒanʲa!]

Socializing

Why are you sad?	**Чому ви засмучені?** [tʃoˈmu wɨ zasˈmutʃɛni?]
Smile! Cheer up!	**Посміхніться!** [posmihˈnitʲsʲa!]
Are you free tonight?	**Ви не зайняті сьогодні ввечері?** [wɨ nɛ ˈzajnʲati sʲoˈɦɔdni ˈwwɛtʃɛri?]
May I offer you a drink?	**Чи можу я запропонувати вам випити?** [tʃɨ ˈmɔʒu ja zaproponuˈwatɨ wam ˈwɨpɨtɨ?]
Would you like to dance?	**Чи не хочете потанцювати?** [tʃɨ nɛ ˈhɔtʃɛtɛ potantsʲuˈwatɨ?]
Let's go to the movies.	**Може сходимо в кіно?** [ˈmɔʒɛ ˈshɔdɨmo w kiˈnɔ?]
May I invite you to …?	**Чи можна запросити вас в …?** [tʃɨ ˈmɔʒna zaproˈsɨtɨ was w …?]
a restaurant	**ресторан** [rɛstoˈran]
the movies	**кіно** [kiˈnɔ]
the theater	**театр** [tɛˈatr]
go for a walk	**на прогулянку** [na proˈɦulʲanku]
At what time?	**О котрій?** [o kotˈrij?]
tonight	**сьогодні ввечері** [sʲoˈɦɔdni ˈwwɛtʃɛri]
at six	**о 6 годині** [o ˈʃɔstij ɦoˈdɨni]
at seven	**о 7 годині** [o ˈsʲɔmij ɦoˈdɨni]
at eight	**о 8 годині** [o ˈwɔsʲmij ɦoˈdɨni]
at nine	**о 9 годині** [o dɛˈwʲʲatij ɦoˈdɨni]
Do you like it here?	**Вам тут подобається?** [wam tut poˈdɔbaɛtʲsʲa?]
Are you here with someone?	**Ви тут з кимось?** [wɨ tut z ˈkɨmosʲ?]

I'm with my friend.
Я з другом /подругою/.
[ja z 'druɦom /'pɔdruɦoʲu/.]

I'm with my friends.
Я з друзями.
[ja z 'druzʲamɨ.]

No, I'm alone.
Я один /одна/.
[ja o'dɨn /od'na/.]

Do you have a boyfriend?
У тебе є приятель?
[u 'tɛbɛ ɛ 'prijatɛlʲ?]

I have a boyfriend.
У мене є друг.
[u 'mɛnɛ ɛ druɦ.]

Do you have a girlfriend?
У тебе є подружка?
[u 'tɛbɛ ɛ 'pɔdruʒka?]

I have a girlfriend.
У мене є дівчина.
[u 'mɛnɛ ɛ 'diwtʃina.]

Can I see you again?
Ми ще зустрінемося?
[mɨ ɕɛ zu'strinɛmosʲa?]

Can I call you?
Чи можна тобі подзвонити?
[tʃi 'mɔʒna to'bi zatɛlɛfonu'wati?]

Call me. (Give me a call.)
Подзвони мені.
[podzwo'nɨ mɛ'ni.]

What's your number?
Який у тебе номер?
[ja'kij u 'tɛbɛ 'nɔmɛr?]

I miss you.
Я сумую за тобою.
[ja su'muʲu za to'bɔʲu.]

You have a beautiful name.
У вас дуже гарне ім'я.
[u was 'duʒɛ 'ɦarnɛ i'mʲʲa.]

I love you.
Я тебе кохаю.
[ja tɛbɛ ko'haʲu.]

Will you marry me?
Виходь за мене.
[wɨ'ɦɔdʲ za 'mɛnɛ.]

You're kidding!
Ви жартуєте!
[wɨ ʒar'tuɛtɛ!]

I'm just kidding.
Я просто жартую.
[ja 'prɔsto ʒar'tuʲu.]

Are you serious?
Ви серйозно?
[wɨ sɛrʲjɔzno?]

I'm serious.
Я серйозно.
[ja sɛrʲjɔzno.]

Really?!
Справді?!
['sprawdi?!]

It's unbelievable!
Це неймовірно!
[tsɛ nɛjmo'wirno]

I don't believe you.
Я вам не вірю.
[ja wam nɛ 'wirʲu.]

I can't.
Я не можу.
[ja nɛ 'mɔʒu.]

I don't know.
Я не знаю.
[ja nɛ 'znaʲu.]

I don't understand you.	**Я вас не розумію.** [ja was nɛ rozu'miʲu.]
Please go away.	**Ідіть, будь ласка.** [i'ditʲ, budʲ 'laska.]
Leave me alone!	**Залиште мене в спокої!** [za'liʃtɛ mɛ'nɛ w 'spɔkoi!]

I can't stand him.	**Я його терпіти не можу.** [ja ʲo'ɦɔ tɛr'pitɨ nɛ 'mɔʒu.]
You are disgusting!	**Ви огидні!** [wɨ o'ɦɨdni!]
I'll call the police!	**Я викличу поліцію!** [ja 'wɨklɨtʃu po'litsʲiʲu!]

Sharing impressions. Emotions

I like it.	**Мені це подобається.** [mɛ'ni tsɛ po'dɔbaɛtʲsʲa.]
Very nice.	**Дуже мило.** ['duʒɛ 'mɨlo.]
That's great!	**Це чудово!** [tsɛ ʧu'dɔwo!]
It's not bad.	**Це непогано.** [tsɛ nɛpo'ɦano.]
I don't like it.	**Мені це не подобається.** [mɛ'ni tsɛ nɛ po'dɔbaɛtʲsʲa.]
It's not good.	**Це недобре.** [tsɛ nɛ'dɔbrɛ.]
It's bad.	**Це погано.** [tsɛ po'ɦano.]
It's very bad.	**Це дуже погано.** [tsɛ 'duʒɛ po'ɦano.]
It's disgusting.	**Це огидно.** [tsɛ o'ɦɨdno.]
I'm happy.	**Я щасливий /щаслива/.** [ja ɕas'lɨwɨj /ɕas'lɨwa/.]
I'm content.	**Я задоволений /задоволена/.** [ja zado'wolɛnɨj /zado'wolɛna/.]
I'm in love.	**Я закоханий /закохана/.** [ja za'kɔhanɨj /za'kɔhana/.]
I'm calm.	**Я спокійний /спокійна/.** [ja spo'kijnɨj /spo'kijna/.]
I'm bored.	**Мені нудно.** [mɛ'ni 'nudno.]
I'm tired.	**Я втомився /втомилася/.** [ja wto'mɨwsʲa /wto'mɨlasʲa/.]
I'm sad.	**Мені сумно.** [mɛ'ni 'sumno.]
I'm frightened.	**Я наляканий /налякана/.** [ja na'lʲakanɨj /na'lʲakana/.]
I'm angry.	**Я злюся.** [ja 'zlʲusʲa.]
I'm worried.	**Я хвилююся.** [ja hwɨ'lʲuʲusʲa.]
I'm nervous.	**Я нервую.** [ja nɛr'wuʲu.]

I'm jealous. (envious)

Я заздрю.
[ja 'zazdrʲu.]

I'm surprised.

Я здивований /здивована/.
[ja zdɨ'wɔwanɨj /zdɨ'wɔwana/.]

I'm perplexed.

Я спантеличений /спантеличена/.
[ja spantɛ'lɨʧɛnɨj /spantɛ'lɨʧɛna/.]

Problems. Accidents

I've got a problem.

В мене проблема.
[w 'mɛnɛ prob'lɛma.]

We've got a problem.

У нас проблема.
[u nas prob'lɛma.]

I'm lost.

Я заблукав /заблукала/.
[ja zablu'kaw /zablu'kala/.]

I missed the last bus (train).

Я запізнився на останній автобус (поїзд).
[ja zapiz'niwsʲa na os'tanij aw'tɔbus ('pɔizd).]

I don't have any money left.

У мене зовсім не залишилося грошей.
[u 'mɛnɛ 'zɔwsim nɛ za'lɨ'ʃilosʲa 'ɦrɔʃɛj.]

I've lost my ...

Я загубив /загубила/ ...
[ja zaɦu'biw /zaɦu'bila/ ...]

Someone stole my ...

В мене вкрали ...
[w 'mɛnɛ 'wkralɨ ...]

passport

паспорт
['pasport]

wallet

гаманець
[ɦama'nɛʦ]

papers

документи
[dokʉ'mɛntɨ]

ticket

квиток
[kwɨ'tɔk]

money

гроші
['ɦrɔʃi]

handbag

сумку
['sumku]

camera

фотоапарат
[fotoapa'rat]

laptop

ноутбук
[nout'buk]

tablet computer

планшет
[plan'ʃɛt]

mobile phone

телефон
[tɛlɛ'fɔn]

Help me!

Допоможіть!
[dopomo'ʒitʲ]

What's happened?

Що трапилося?
[ɕo 'trapɨlosʲa?]

---

fire	**пожежа** [po'ʒɛʒa]
shooting	**стрілянина** [strilʲa'nɨna]
murder	**вбивство** ['wbɨwstwo]
explosion	**вибух** ['wɨbuh]
fight	**бійка** ['bijka]

Call the police!	**Викличте поліцію!** ['wɨklɨʧtɛ po'litsʲiʲu!]
Please hurry up!	**Будь ласка, швидше!** [budʲ 'laska, 'ʃwɨdʃɛ!]
I'm looking for the police station.	**Я шукаю поліцейську дільницю.** [ja ʃu'kaʲu poli'tsɛjsʲku dilʲ'nɨtsʲu.]
I need to make a call.	**Мені треба зателефонувати.** [mɛ'ni 'trɛba zatɛlɛfonu'watɨ.]
May I use your phone?	**Чи можна мені зателефонувати?** [ʧɨ 'mɔʒna mɛ'ni zatɛlɛfonu'watɨ?]

I've been …	**Мене …** [mɛ'nɛ …]
mugged	**пограбували** [poɦrabu'walɨ]
robbed	**обікрали** [obi'kralɨ]
raped	**зґвалтували** [zgwaltu'walɨ]
attacked (beaten up)	**побили** [po'bɨlɨ]

Are you all right?	**З вами все гаразд?** [z 'wamɨ wsɛ ɦa'razd?]
Did you see who it was?	**Ви бачили, хто це був?** [wɨ 'baʧɨlɨ, hto tsɛ buw?]
Would you be able to recognize the person?	**Ви зможете його впізнати?** [wɨ 'zmɔʒɛtɛ ʲo'ɦɔ wpiz'natɨ?]
Are you sure?	**Ви точно впевнені?** [wɨ 'tɔʧno 'wpɛwnɛni?]

Please calm down.	**Будь ласка, заспокойтеся.** [budʲ 'laska, zaspo'kɔjtɛsʲa.]
Take it easy!	**Спокійніше!** [spokij'niʃɛ!]
Don't worry!	**Не турбуйтесь.** [nɛ tur'bujtɛsʲ.]
Everything will be fine.	**Все буде добре.** [wsɛ 'budɛ 'dobrɛ.]
Everything's all right.	**Все гаразд.** [wsɛ ɦa'razd.]

Come here, please.

Підійдіть, будь ласка.
[pidij'ditʲ, budʲ 'laska.]

I have some questions for you.

У мене до вас кілька запитань.
[u 'mɛnɛ do was 'kilʲka zapɨ'tanʲ.]

Wait a moment, please.

Зачекайте, будь ласка.
[zatʃɛ'kajtɛ, budʲ 'laska.]

Do you have any I.D.?

У вас є документи?
[u was 'ɛ doku'mɛntɨ?]

Thanks. You can leave now.

Дякую. Ви можете йти.
['dʲakuʲu. wɨ 'mɔʒɛtɛ jtɨ.]

Hands behind your head!

Руки за голову!
['rukɨ za 'ɦɔlowu!]

You're under arrest!

Ви заарештовані!
[wɨ zaarɛʃ'tɔwani!]

Health problems

Please help me.	**Допоможіть, будь ласка.** [dopomo'ʒitʲ, budʲ 'laska.]
I don't feel well.	**Мені погано.** [mɛ'ni po'ɦano.]
My husband doesn't feel well.	**Моєму чоловікові погано.** [mo'ɛmu ʧolo'wikowi po'ɦano.]
My son …	**Моєму сину …** [mo'ɛmu 'sɨnu …]
My father …	**Моєму батькові …** [mo'ɛmu 'batʲkowi …]

My wife doesn't feel well.	**Моїй дружині погано.** [mo'ij dru'ʒɨni po'ɦano.]
My daughter …	**Моїй дочці …** [mo'ij doʧ'tsi …]
My mother …	**Моїй матері …** [mo'ij 'matɛri …]

I've got a …	**У мене болить …** [u 'mɛnɛ bo'lɨtʲ …]
headache	**голова** [ɦolo'wa]
sore throat	**горло** ['ɦɔrlo]
stomach ache	**живіт** [ʒɨ'wit]
toothache	**зуб** [zub]

I feel dizzy.	**У мене паморочиться голова.** [u 'mɛnɛ 'pamoroʧɨtʲsʲa ɦolo'wa.]
He has a fever.	**У нього температура.** [u 'nʲoɦo tɛmpɛra'tura.]
She has a fever.	**У неї температура.** [u nɛi tɛmpɛra'tura.]
I can't breathe.	**Я не можу дихати.** [ja nɛ 'mɔʒu 'dɨhatɨ.]

I'm short of breath.	**Я задихаюсь.** [ja zadɨ'haʲusʲ.]
I am asthmatic.	**Я астматик.** [ja ast'matɨk.]
I am diabetic.	**Я діабетик.** [ja dia'bɛtɨk.]

I can't sleep.
В мене безсоння.
[w 'mɛnɛ bɛz'sɔnʲa.]

food poisoning
харчове отруєння
[hartʃo'wɛ ot'ruɛnʲa]

It hurts here.
Болить ось тут.
[bo'litʲ osʲ tut.]

Help me!
Допоможіть!
[dopomo'ʒitʲ!]

I am here!
Я тут!
[ja tut!]

We are here!
Ми тут!
[mɨ tut!]

Get me out of here!
Витягніть мене!
['witʲaɦnitʲ mɛ'nɛ!]

I need a doctor.
Мені потрібен лікар.
[mɛ'ni po'tribɛn 'likar.]

I can't move.
Я не можу рухатися.
[ja nɛ 'mɔʒu 'ruhatisʲa.]

I can't move my legs.
Я не відчуваю ніг.
[ja nɛ widtʃu'waʲu niɦ.]

I have a wound.
Я поранений /поранена/.
[ja po'ranɛnij /po'ranɛna/.]

Is it serious?
Це серйозно?
[tsɛ sɛr'jɔzno?]

My documents are in my pocket.
Мої документи в кишені.
[mo'i doku'mɛnti w ki'ʃɛni.]

Calm down!
Заспокойтеся!
[zaspo'kɔjtɛsʲa!]

May I use your phone?
Чи можна мені зателефонувати?
[tʃi 'mɔʒna mɛ'ni zatɛlɛfonu'wati?]

Call an ambulance!
Викличте швидку!
['wiklitʃtɛ ʃwid'ku!]

It's urgent!
Це терміново!
[tsɛ tɛrmi'nɔwo!]

It's an emergency!
Це дуже терміново!
[tsɛ 'duʒɛ tɛrmi'nɔwo!]

Please hurry up!
Будь ласка, швидше!
[budʲ 'laska, 'ʃwidʃɛ!]

Would you please call a doctor?
Викличте лікаря, будь ласка.
['wiklitʃtɛ 'likarʲa, budʲ 'laska.]

Where is the hospital?
Скажіть, де лікарня?
[ska'ʒitʲ, dɛ li'karnʲa?]

How are you feeling?
Як ви себе почуваєте?
[jak wɨ sɛ'bɛ potʃu'waɛtɛ?]

Are you all right?
З вами все гаразд?
[z 'wami wsɛ ɦa'razd?]

What's happened?
Що трапилося?
[ɕo 'trapilosʲa?]

I feel better now.

Мені вже краще.
[mɛ'ni wʒɛ 'kraɕɛ.]

It's OK.

Все гаразд.
[wsɛ ɦa'razd.]

It's all right.

Все добре.
[wsɛ 'dɔbrɛ.]

At the pharmacy

pharmacy (drugstore)	**аптека** [ap'tɛka]
24-hour pharmacy	**цілодобова аптека** [ʦilodo'bowa ap'tɛka]
Where is the closest pharmacy?	**Де найближча аптека?** [dɛ najb'liʒʧa ap'tɛka?]
Is it open now?	**Вона зараз відкрита?** [wo'na 'zaraz wid'krita?]
At what time does it open?	**О котрій вона відкривається?** [o kot'rij wo'na widkriˡwaɛtˡsⁱa?]
At what time does it close?	**До котрої години вона працює?** [do ko'troi ɦo'dini wo'na praˡʦⁱuɛ?]
Is it far?	**Це далеко?** [ʦɛ da'lɛko?]
Can I get there on foot?	**Я дійду туди пішки?** [ja dij'du tu'di 'piʃki?]
Can you show me on the map?	**Покажіть мені на карті, будь ласка.** [poka'ʒitⁱ mɛ'ni na 'karti, budⁱ 'laska.]
Please give me something for ...	**Дайте мені, що-небудь від ...** ['dajtɛ mɛ'ni, ɕo-'nɛbudⁱ wid ...]
a headache	**головного болю** [ɦolow'noɦo 'bolⁱu]
a cough	**кашлю** ['kaʃlⁱu]
a cold	**застуди** [za'studi]
the flu	**грипу** ['ɦripu]
a fever	**температури** [tɛmpɛra'turi]
a stomach ache	**болю в шлунку** ['bolⁱu w 'ʃlunku]
nausea	**нудоти** [nu'doti]
diarrhea	**діареї** [dia'rɛi]
constipation	**запору** [za'poru]
pain in the back	**біль у спині** ['bilⁱ u spi'ni]

chest pain	**біль у грудях** ['bilʲ u 'ɦrudʲah]
side stitch	**біль у боці** ['bilʲ u 'bɔʦi]
abdominal pain	**біль в животі** ['bilʲ w ʒiwo'ti]

pill	**таблетка** [tab'lɛtka]
ointment, cream	**мазь, крем** [mazʲ, krɛm]
syrup	**сироп** [sɨ'rɔp]
spray	**спрей** ['sprɛj]
drops	**краплі** ['krapli]

You need to go to the hospital.	**Вам потрібно в лікарню.** [wam po'tribno w li'karnʲu.]
health insurance	**страховка** [stra'hɔwka]
prescription	**рецепт** [rɛ'ʦɛpt]
insect repellant	**засіб від комах** ['zasib wid ko'mah]
Band Aid	**лейкопластир** [lɛjko'plastɨr]

The bare minimum

Excuse me, ...	**Вибачте, ...** ['wɨbatʃtɛ, ...]
Hello.	**Добрий день.** ['dɔbrij dɛnʲ.]
Thank you.	**Дякую.** ['dʲakuʲu.]
Good bye.	**До побачення.** [do poˈbatʃɛnʲa.]
Yes.	**Так.** [tak.]
No.	**Ні.** [ni.]
I don't know.	**Я не знаю.** [ja nɛ ˈznaʲu.]
Where?	Where to?	When?	**Де?	Куди?	Коли?** [dɛ?	kuˈdɨ?	koˈlɨ?]

I need ...	**Мені потрібен ...** [mɛˈni poˈtribɛn ...]
I want ...	**Я хочу ...** [ja ˈhoʧu ...]
Do you have ...?	**У вас є ...?** [u was ˈɛ ...?]
Is there a ... here?	**Тут є ...?** [tut ɛ ...?]
May I ...?	**Чи можна мені ...?** [ʧɨ ˈmɔʒna mɛˈni ...?]
..., please (polite request)	**Будь ласка** [budʲ ˈlaska]

I'm looking for ...	**Я шукаю ...** [ja ʃuˈkaʲu ...]
restroom	**туалет** [tuaˈlɛt]
ATM	**банкомат** [bankoˈmat]
pharmacy (drugstore)	**аптеку** [apˈtɛku]
hospital	**лікарню** [liˈkarnʲu]
police station	**поліцейську дільницю** [poliˈtsɛjsʲku dilʲˈnitsʲu]
subway	**метро** [mɛtˈrɔ]

| taxi | **таксі**
[tak'si] |
| train station | **вокзал**
[wok'zal] |

My name is …	**Мене звуть …** [mɛ'nɛ zwutʲ …]
What's your name?	**Як вас звуть?** [jak was 'zwutʲ?]
Could you please help me?	**Допоможіть мені, будь ласка.** [dopomo'ʒitʲ mɛ'ni, budʲ 'laska.]
I've got a problem.	**У мене проблема.** [u 'mɛnɛ prob'lɛma.]
I don't feel well.	**Мені погано.** [mɛ'ni po'ɦano.]
Call an ambulance!	**Викличте швидку!** ['wiklitʃtɛ ʃwid'ku!]
May I make a call?	**Чи можна мені зателефонувати?** [tʃɨ 'mɔʒna mɛ'ni zatɛlɛfonu'wati?]

| I'm sorry. | **Прошу вибачення**
['prɔʃu 'wibatʃɛnʲa] |
| You're welcome. | **Прошу**
['prɔʃu] |

I, me	**я** [ja]
you (inform.)	**ти** [tɨ]
he	**він** [win]
she	**вона** [wo'na]
they (masc.)	**вони** [wo'nɨ]
they (fem.)	**вони** [wo'nɨ]
we	**ми** [mɨ]
you (pl)	**ви** [wɨ]
you (sg, form.)	**Ви** [wɨ]

ENTRANCE	**ВХІД** [whid]
EXIT	**ВИХІД** ['wihid]
OUT OF ORDER	**НЕ ПРАЦЮЄ** [nɛ pra'tsʲuɛ]
CLOSED	**ЗАКРИТО** [za'krito]

OPEN   **ВІДКРИТО**
[wid'krito]

FOR WOMEN   **ДЛЯ ЖІНОК**
[dlʲa ʒi'nɔk]

FOR MEN   **ДЛЯ ЧОЛОВІКІВ**
[dlʲa tʃolowi'kiw]

MINI DICTIONARY

This section contains 250
useful words required for
everyday communication.
You will find the names of
months and days of the week
here. The dictionary also
contains topics such as colors,
measurements, family, and
more

T&P Books Publishing

DICTIONARY CONTENTS

T&P Books Publishing

time	час (с)	[ʧas]
hour	година (ж)	[ɦoʹdina]
half an hour	півгодини (мн)	[piwɦoʹdini]
minute	хвилина (ж)	[hwiʹlina]
second	секунда (ж)	[sɛʹkunda]
today (adv)	сьогодні	[sʲoʹɦɔdni]
tomorrow (adv)	завтра	[ʹzawtra]
yesterday (adv)	вчора	[ʹwʧɔra]
Monday	понеділок (ч)	[pɔnɛʹdilok]
Tuesday	вівторок (ч)	[wiwʹtɔrok]
Wednesday	середа (ж)	[sɛrɛʹda]
Thursday	четвер (ч)	[ʧɛtʹwɛr]
Friday	п'ятниця (ж)	[ʹpʲatnitsʲa]
Saturday	субота (ж)	[suʹbɔta]
Sunday	неділя (ж)	[nɛʹdilʲa]
day	день (ч)	[dɛnʲ]
working day	робочий день (ч)	[roʹbɔʧij dɛnʲ]
public holiday	святковий день (ч)	[swʲatʹkɔwij dɛnʲ]
weekend	вихідні (мн)	[wiɦidʹni]
week	тиждень (ч)	[ʹtiʒdɛnʲ]
last week (adv)	на минулому тижні	[na miʹnulomu ʹtiʒni]
next week (adv)	на наступному тижні	[na naʹstupnomu ʹtiʒni]
in the morning	вранці	[ʹwrantsi]
in the afternoon	після обіду	[ʹpislʲa oʹbidu]
in the evening	увечері	[uʹwɛʧɛri]
tonight (this evening)	сьогодні увечері	[sʲoʹɦɔdni uʹwɛʧɛri]
at night	уночі	[unoʹʧi]
midnight	північ (ж)	[ʹpiwniʧ]
January	січень (ч)	[ʹsiʧɛnʲ]
February	лютий (ч)	[ʹlʲutij]
March	березень (ч)	[ʹbɛrɛzɛnʲ]
April	квітень (ч)	[ʹkwitɛnʲ]
May	травень (ч)	[ʹtrawɛnʲ]
June	червень (ч)	[ʹʧɛrwɛnʲ]
July	липень (ч)	[ʹlipɛnʲ]
August	серпень (ч)	[ʹsɛrpɛnʲ]

September	вересень (ч)	[ˈwɛrɛsɛnʲ]
October	жовтень (ч)	[ˈʒɔwtɛnʲ]
November	листопад (ч)	[lisˈtoˈpad]
December	грудень (ч)	[ˈɦrudɛnʲ]

in spring	навесні	[nawɛsˈni]
in summer	влітку	[ˈwlitku]
in fall	восени	[wosɛˈnɨ]
in winter	взимку	[ˈwzɨmku]

month	місяць (ч)	[ˈmisʲats]
season (summer, etc.)	сезон (ч)	[sɛˈzɔn]
year	рік (ч)	[rik]

2. Numbers. Numerals

0 zero	нуль	[nulʲ]
1 one	один	[oˈdɨn]
2 two	два	[dwa]
3 three	три	[tri]
4 four	чотири	[ʧoˈtɨri]

5 five	п'ять	[pʲatʲ]
6 six	шість	[ʃistʲ]
7 seven	сім	[sim]
8 eight	вісім	[ˈwisim]
9 nine	дев'ять	[ˈdɛwʲatʲ]
10 ten	десять	[ˈdɛsʲatʲ]

11 eleven	одинадцять	[odiˈnadtsʲatʲ]
12 twelve	дванадцять	[dwaˈnadtsʲatʲ]
13 thirteen	тринадцять	[triˈnadtsʲatʲ]
14 fourteen	чотирнадцять	[ʧotirˈnadtsʲatʲ]
15 fifteen	п'ятнадцять	[pʲatˈnadtsʲatʲ]

16 sixteen	шістнадцять	[ʃistˈnadtsʲatʲ]
17 seventeen	сімнадцять	[simˈnadtsʲatʲ]
18 eighteen	вісімнадцять	[wisimˈnadtsʲatʲ]
19 nineteen	дев'ятнадцять	[dɛwʲatˈnadtsʲatʲ]

20 twenty	двадцять	[ˈdwadtsʲatʲ]
30 thirty	тридцять	[ˈtridtsʲatʲ]
40 forty	сорок	[ˈsɔrok]
50 fifty	п'ятдесят	[pʲatdɛˈsʲat]

60 sixty	шістдесят	[ʃizdɛˈsʲat]
70 seventy	сімдесят	[simdɛˈsʲat]
80 eighty	вісімдесят	[wisimdɛˈsʲat]
90 ninety	дев'яносто	[dɛwʲaˈnɔsto]
100 one hundred	сто	[sto]

200 two hundred	двісті	['dwisti]
300 three hundred	триста	['trista]
400 four hundred	чотириста	[ʧo'tirista]
500 five hundred	п'ятсот	[pʲa'tsɔt]

600 six hundred	шістсот	[ʃist'sɔt]
700 seven hundred	сімсот	[sim'sɔt]
800 eight hundred	вісімсот	[wisim'sɔt]
900 nine hundred	дев'ятсот	[dɛwʲa'tsɔt]
1000 one thousand	тисяча	['tisʲaʧa]

| 10000 ten thousand | десять тисяч | ['dɛsʲatʲ 'tisʲaʧ] |
| one hundred thousand | сто тисяч | [sto 'tisʲaʧ] |

| million | мільйон (ч) | [milʲʲjon] |
| billion | мільярд (ч) | [mi'ljard] |

3. Humans. Family

man (adult male)	чоловік (ч)	[ʧolo'wik]
young man	юнак (ч)	[ʲu'nak]
woman	жінка (ж)	['ʒinka]
girl (young woman)	дівчина (ж)	['diwʧina]
old man	старий (ч)	[sta'rij]
old woman	стара (ж)	[sta'ra]

mother	мати (ж)	['mati]
father	батько (ч)	['batʲko]
son	син (ч)	[sin]
daughter	дочка (ж)	[doʧ'ka]
brother	брат (ч)	[brat]
sister	сестра (ж)	[sɛst'ra]

parents	батьки (мн)	[batʲʲki]
child	дитина (ж)	[di'tina]
children	діти (мн)	['diti]
stepmother	мачуха (ж)	['maʧuha]
stepfather	вітчим (ч)	['witʧim]

grandmother	бабуся (ж)	[ba'busʲa]
grandfather	дід (ч)	['did]
grandson	онук (ч)	[o'nuk]
granddaughter	онука (ж)	[o'nuka]
grandchildren	онуки (мн)	[o'nuki]

uncle	дядько (ч)	['dʲadʲko]
aunt	тітка (ж)	['titka]
nephew	племінник (ч)	[plɛ'minik]
niece	племінниця (ж)	[plɛ'minitsʲa]
wife	дружина (ж)	[dru'ʒina]

husband	чоловік (ч)	[tʃolo'wik]
married (masc.)	одружений	[od'ruʒenij]
married (fem.)	заміжня	[za'miʒnʲa]
widow	вдова (ж)	[wdo'wa]
widower	вдівець (ч)	[wdi'wɛts]

| name (first name) | ім'я (с) | [i'mʲa] |
| surname (last name) | прізвище (с) | ['prizwiҫɛ] |

relative	родич (ч)	['rɔditʃ]
friend (masc.)	товариш (ч)	[to'wariʃ]
friendship	дружба (ж)	['druʒba]

partner	партнер (ч)	[part'nɛr]
superior (n)	начальник (ч)	[na'tʃalʲnɨk]
colleague	колега (ч)	[ko'lɛɦa]
neighbors	сусіди (мн)	[su'sidɨ]

4. Human body

body	тіло (с)	['tilo]
heart	серце (с)	['sɛrtsɛ]
blood	кров (ж)	[krow]
brain	мозок (ч)	['mɔzok]

bone	кістка (ж)	['kistka]
spine (backbone)	хребет (ч)	[hrɛ'bɛt]
rib	ребро (с)	[rɛb'rɔ]
lungs	легені (мн)	[lɛ'ɦɛni]
skin	шкіра (ж)	['ʃkira]

head	голова (ж)	[ɦolo'wa]
face	обличчя (с)	[ob'litʃʲa]
nose	ніс (ч)	[nis]
forehead	чоло (с)	[tʃo'lɔ]
cheek	щока (ж)	[ҫo'ka]

mouth	рот (ч)	[rot]
tongue	язик (ч)	[ja'zik]
tooth	зуб (ч)	[zub]
lips	губи (мн)	['ɦubɨ]
chin	підборіддя (с)	[pidbo'riddʲa]

ear	вухо (с)	['wuho]
neck	шия (ж)	['ʃʲa]
eye	око (с)	['ɔko]
pupil	зіниця (ч)	[zi'nɨtsʲa]
eyebrow	брова (ж)	[bro'wa]
eyelash	вія (ж)	['wiʲa]
hair	волосся (с)	[wo'lɔssʲa]

hairstyle	зачіска (ж)	['zatʃiska]
mustache	вуса (мн)	['wusa]
beard	борода (ж)	[boro'da]
to have (a beard, etc.)	носити	[no'siti]
bald (adj)	лисий	['lisij]

hand	кисть (ж)	[kistʲ]
arm	рука (ж)	[ru'ka]
finger	палець (ч)	['palɛts]
nail	ніготь (ч)	['nihotʲ]
palm	долоня (ж)	[do'lonʲa]

shoulder	плече (с)	[plɛ'tʃɛ]
leg	гомілка (ж)	[ɦo'milka]
knee	коліно (с)	[ko'lino]
heel	п'ятка (ж)	['pʲatka]
back	спина (ж)	['spina]

5. Clothing. Personal accessories

clothes	одяг (ч)	['ɔdʲaɦ]
coat (overcoat)	пальто (с)	[palʲ'to]
fur coat	шуба (ж)	['ʃuba]
jacket (e.g., leather ~)	куртка (ж)	['kurtka]
raincoat (trenchcoat, etc.)	плащ (ч)	[plaɕ]

shirt (button shirt)	сорочка (ж)	[so'rɔtʃka]
pants	штани (мн)	[ʃta'ni]
suit jacket	піджак (ч)	[pi'dʒak]
suit	костюм (ч)	[kos'tʲum]

dress (frock)	сукня (ж)	['suknʲa]
skirt	спідниця (ж)	[spid'nitsʲa]
T-shirt	футболка (ж)	[fut'bolka]
bathrobe	халат (ч)	[ha'lat]
pajamas	піжама (ж)	[pi'ʒama]
workwear	робочий одяг (ж)	[ro'botʃij 'ɔdʲaɦ]

underwear	білизна (ж)	[bi'lizna]
socks	шкарпетки (мн)	[ʃkar'pɛtki]
bra	бюстгальтер (ч)	[bʲust'ɦalʲtɛr]
pantyhose	колготки (мн)	[kol'ɦotki]
stockings (thigh highs)	панчохи (мн)	[pan'tʃɔhi]
bathing suit	купальник (ч)	[ku'palʲnik]

hat	шапка (ж)	['ʃapka]
footwear	взуття (с)	[wzut'tʲa]
boots (e.g., cowboy ~)	чоботи (мн)	['tʃoboti]
heel	каблук (ч)	[kab'luk]
shoestring	шнурок (ч)	[ʃnu'rɔk]

shoe polish	крем (ч) для взуття	[krɛm dlʲa wzutʲtʲa]
gloves	рукавички (мн)	[ruka'witʃki]
mittens	рукавиці (мн)	[ruka'witsi]
scarf (muffler)	шарф (ч)	[ʃarf]
glasses (eyeglasses)	окуляри (мн)	[oku'lʲari]
umbrella	парасолька (ж)	[para'solʲka]

tie (necktie)	краватка (ж)	[kra'watka]
handkerchief	носовичок (ч)	[nosowi'tʃok]
comb	гребінець (ч)	[hrɛbi'nɛts]
hairbrush	щітка (ж) для волосся	['ɕitka dlʲa wo'lossʲa]

buckle	пряжка (ж)	['prʲaʒka]
belt	пасок (ч)	['pasok]
purse	сумочка (ж)	['sumotʃka]

6. House. Apartment

apartment	квартира (ж)	[kwar'tira]
room	кімната (ж)	[kim'nata]
bedroom	спальня (ж)	['spalʲnʲa]
dining room	їдальня (ж)	['jidalʲnʲa]

living room	вітальня (ж)	[wi'talʲnʲa]
study (home office)	кабінет (ч)	[kabi'nɛt]
entry room	передпокій (ч)	[pɛrɛd'pokij]
bathroom (room with a bath or shower)	ванна кімната (ж)	['wana kim'nata]
half bath	туалет (ч)	[tua'lɛt]

vacuum cleaner	пилосос (ч)	[piło'sɔs]
mop	швабра (ж)	['ʃwabra]
dust cloth	ганчірка (ж)	[han'tʃirka]
short broom	віник (ч)	['winik]
dustpan	совок (ч) для сміття	[so'wɔk dlʲa smit'tʲa]

furniture	меблі (мн)	['mɛbli]
table	стіл (ч)	[stil]
chair	стілець (ч)	[sti'lɛts]
armchair	крісло (с)	['krislo]

mirror	дзеркало (с)	['dzɛrkało]
carpet	килим (ч)	['kiłim]
fireplace	камін (ч)	[ka'min]
drapes	штори (мн)	['ʃtɔri]
table lamp	настільна лампа (ж)	[na'stilʲna 'lampa]
chandelier	люстра (ж)	['lʲustra]

kitchen	кухня (ж)	['kuhnʲa]
gas stove (range)	плита (ж) газова	[plʲi'ta 'hazowa]

electric stove	плита (ж) електрична	[plɨ'ta ɛlɛkt'ritʃna]
microwave oven	мікрохвильова піч (ж)	[mikrohwɨlʲo'wa pitʃ]
refrigerator	холодильник (ч)	[holo'dɨlʲnɨk]
freezer	морозильник (ч)	[moro'zɨlʲnɨk]
dishwasher	посудомийна машина (ж)	[posudo'mɨjna ma'ʃina]
faucet	кран (ч)	[kran]
meat grinder	м'ясорубка (ж)	[mʲaso'rubka]
juicer	соковижималка (ж)	[sokowɨʒɨ'malka]
toaster	тостер (ч)	['tɔstɛr]
mixer	міксер (ч)	['miksɛr]
coffee machine	кавоварка (ж)	[kawo'warka]
kettle	чайник (ч)	['tʃajnɨk]
teapot	заварник (ч)	[za'warnɨk]
TV set	телевізор (ч)	[tɛlɛ'wizor]
VCR (video recorder)	відеомагнітофон (ч)	['widɛo mafinito'fɔn]
iron (e.g., steam ~)	праска (ж)	['praska]
telephone	телефон (ч)	[tɛlɛ'fɔn]

Lightning Source UK Ltd.
Milton Keynes UK
UKHW022018130522
402975UK00006B/1205